This Book Belongs to

_____

_____

AN ABC BESTIARY

Deborah Blackwell

FARRAR · STRAUS · GIROUX
NEW YORK

FOR TOM

A FLOYD YEAROUT BOOK
316 Wellesley Street
Weston, Massachusetts 02193

Library of Congress catalog card number: 89-45504
Published simultaneously in Canada by Collins Publishers, Toronto
Production coordinated by Trilogy, Milan
Color separations by Sele Color
Printed in Italy by Mazzucchelli
Bound in Italy by Olivotto
Designed by Deborah Blackwell
First edition, 1989

Aardvark arranging art

B b

Bear bouncing berries

C c

Chicken cooking croissants

D d

Dinosaur dialing dentist

Ee

Elephant exploring Ecuador

F f

Frog fixing flat

G g

Goat growing gladiolas

H h

Herring harassing heron

I i

Iguana interpreting irises

J j

Jaguar juggling jellybeans

K k

Kangaroo keeping kittens

L l

Lynx lifting lure

M m

Moose mimicking maestro

N n

Newt nibbling noodles

Otter orbiting Orion

Python playing prank

Q q

Quail quitting quilting

Rr

Rabbit reading rebus

S s

Seal savoring sushi

T t

Terrier trimming topiary

U u

Unicorn undertaking U-turn

V v

Vixen vending vegetables

W w

Wasps wearing waistcoats

X x Y y Z z

X-marked Yak Zooming